D1549267

WHAT'S YOUR VIEW ?

THE POWER OF THE MEDIA

Adam Hibbert

W
FRANKLIN WATTS
LONDON•SYDNEY

First published in 2006 by
Franklin Watts
338 Euston Road
London NW1 3BH

Franklin Watts Australia
Level 17/207 Kent Street
Sydney NSW 2000

ISBN: 0 7496 6306 5
Dewey Classification: 302.23

Series editor: Sarah Peutrill
Art director: Jonathan Hair
Design: Proof Books
Picture researcher: Sophie Hartley

Picture and text credits: see page 48.
Every attempt has been made to clear copyright.
Should there be any inadvertent omission please apply
to the publisher for rectification.

Note on quotes: Quotes presented in this book in a
specific context should not be understood to commit
their source to one side of that debate. They are simply
illustrations of the possible viewpoints in each debate.

Note on websites:
Every effort has been made by the Publishers to ensure
that the websites in this book contain no inappropriate
or offensive material. However, because of the nature
of the Internet, it is impossible to guarantee that the
contents of these sites will not be altered. We strongly
advise that Internet access is supervised by a
responsible adult.

A CIP catalogue record for this book is available from
the British Library.

Printed in China

Contents

4   What's the issue?

6   Is free speech good for us?

8   Do consumer choices influence the media?

10 Does the media influence democratic decisions?

12 Does the concentration of media under a few owners need control?

14 Should public benefit come before profit?

16 Is advertising to children wrong?

18 Should the media report on the private lives of public figures?

20 Should journalists be allowed to keep sources 'off the record'?

22 Is TV to blame for changes in the way families socialise?

24 Do media images of models harm our self-esteem?

26 Does access to government files improve democracy?

28 Is the media responsible for 'personality' politics?

30 Should the media hire more journalists of different classes, genders or cultures?

32 Should the media censor extremists' views?

34 Does violence on screen affect the morals of viewers?

36 Do films need censoring?

38 Does TV news over-simplify complex issues?

40 Should we have TV cameras in courtrooms?

42 Will web media become more powerful than traditional media?

44 Glossary

46 Debating tips

47 Index

48 Acknowledgements

What's the issue?

WHY MEDIA POWER MATTERS

Television, radio, websites, newspapers, magazines, books are all media – they convey information to the public. This information has to be gathered together, edited and presented, and in this process decisions have to be made about what is the most important or most relevant to the audience. For example, music fans can buy a magazine that focuses on music, and excludes politics or sport.

The word 'media' comes from 'middle' – the media stands in the middle, between us and the world.

MEDIA AND VOTERS

In a democracy, every person plays a part in choosing what the nation should do. A democracy needs most of its citizens to be aware of world events, or voters will make poor decisions. The media is the main source of information for most voters. If the media provides poor quality information, voters are more likely to make bad decisions.

'A popular government without popular information, or the means of acquiring it, is but a prologue to a farce or a tragedy, or perhaps both.'
James Madison, a founder of the US constitution, 1822

In a global survey of press freedoms in 2004, Italy lost its top rank because Prime Minister Silvio Berlusconi (pictured) owned or controlled too much of the country's media.

GOOD INFORMATION
Over time, modern societies have developed ways to improve the quality of information in the media:

Freedom of the press
Rules that protect the media from interference by the government, which might try to control the information available to voters.

Multiple ownership
Rules that prevent all the media in a country being owned by one person, or one small group of people, who might control information.

Internet freedom
Rules that protect citizens' access to information on the Internet, especially information from outside their own country.

Freedom of information
Rules that require the government to release information it holds to the public, as far as possible.

Fair advertising
Rules that stop companies giving out false or misleading information in advertisements.

Impartiality
Rules that encourage journalists to be fair to all sides of a political argument when they report a story.

Protection of sources
Rules that allow journalists to refuse to name a person who gave them secret information.

Separation of editorial and advertising
Rules to help consumers trust that the information they see is not influenced or censored by advertisers.

GROWTH IN WORLD ADVERTISING

YEAR	BILLION US$	%CHANGE
1990	275.9	+ 7.9
1991	282.3	+ 2.3
1992	299.2	+ 6.0
1993	304.2	+ 1.7
1994	332.0	+ 9.1
1995	371.0	+ 11.7
1996	390.2	+ 5.2
1997	401.3	+ 2.8
1998	411.9	+ 2.6
1999	436.1	+ 5.9
2000	474.3	+ 8.8
2001	440.9	- 7.9
2002	450.5	+ 2.2
2003	471.1	+ 4.6
2004	498.3	+ 5.8

Universal McCann: The Insider's Report

The power of the media to affect politics is a huge issue, but messages in the media also influence other aspects of our lives. In the following pages, we will explore possible effects on:
- family life
- consumer choices
- children's health
- violent behaviour.

Each debate gives you the opinions of several people or organisations, plus relevant statistics as a starting point for a debate. Conflicting Evidence explores how research may seem to support either side. Each spread concludes with some websites to help you investigate the debate further and begin to decide which side of the debate you agree with. If you wish to take it further and hold a debate on one or more of these issues, check out the debating tips on page 46.

Q: Is free speech good for us?

Heorhiy Gongadze, a Ukrainian journalist who used free speech to expose government corruption, was kidnapped and killed in 2000. The government was suspected of 'silencing' him. In 2004, Ukrainian protesters threw out the old government.

FREEDOM OF speech is an ideal that all governments limit to some extent. For example, information that may upset children has to be distributed carefully. Some countries have also chosen to make publicising certain political or religious views through the media illegal – particularly viewpoints that encourage violence. However, some people say that this suppression of people's viewpoints is a step too far.

YES

'I believe violence is committed by people who feel powerless. They feel like they have no other option than physical force for wielding power in our society. I believe that open publishing gives people a small amount of empowerment to have their views heard and responded to by their community.'

'Stacy', Indymedia moderator, Sydney IMC, in a free speech dispute, Australia

'[To have] democratic debate ... we must have freedom of expression, and the right to publish the truth as we understand it without the threat of being closed down by the courts.'

Mick Hume, editor of LM magazine, UK, closed after a court case

'It's so tempting to think, "Oh, if we just give up our freedoms, then we'll be safe". But nothing can protect us from terrorism. We're never going to be safe in that sense – but at least we can be free.'

Nadine Strossen, president of the American Civil Liberties Union (ACLU)

CONFLICTING EVIDENCE?

'These data show that [hate speech] interactions occur with regularity and leave targets harmed in significant ways ... Although the legal status of hate speech remains ambiguous, its harms are not.'

Laura Beth Nielsen, Subtle, Pervasive, Harmful

Countries banning Holocaust denial	Effect on anti-semitic activities
Austria	none recorded
Belgium	small decline
France	none recorded
Germany	none recorded
Spain	none recorded
Switzerland	small decline
Control (no ban)	
UK	small decline

Source: www.jpr.org.uk

✳ STATISTICALLY SPEAKING

Newspaper use linked with political freedom

Freedom rankings show the level of political rights and civil liberties by country. A ranking of 1 = free, 7 = unfree. The charts show the freedom rankings of countries that have a high and low number of newspapers purchased per person.

Top five countries (most newspapers read per person)
Hong Kong, Norway, Japan, Finland, Sweden, average
Freedom ranking 1 2 3 4 5 6 7

Bottom five countries (fewest newspapers read per person)
Kenya, Zimbabwe, Pakistan, South Africa, Egypt, average
Freedom ranking 1 2 3 4 5 6 7

NO

'The only way to fight hate speech or racist speech is to recognise it as the speech of your enemy, and what you do in response to the speech of your enemy is not prescribe a medication for it but attempt to stamp it out.'

Stanley Fish, There's no such thing as free speech – and it's a good thing, too

✖ 'I'm not an absolute free speech person. I don't believe you can give secrets to the enemy, or urge people to throw bombs, under the guise of free speech ... you can't use free speech to holler "fire" in a crowded theatre.'

Rafe Mair, political commentator, Canada

✖ 'Free speech does not include the right to incite the murder of other human beings. We are campaigning ... explicitly and exclusively against singers who promote the killing of gays and lesbians.'

Peter Tatchell, of the Stop Murder Music campaign, UK

MORE TO THINK ABOUT

On these pages we have seen why freedom of speech may be good for us and when it might not. This book also explores issues where we might want to place controls on the media. For each issue, look out for ways these controls might be misused to harm democracy.

FIND OUT MORE: www.article19.org www.rsf.org
http://stop.censoring.us www.indefenseoffreedom.org

Q: Do consumer choices influence the media?

Most MEDIA producers are businesses, earning money by selling information to their customers. Some people argue that this stops the media having too much power: if consumers find one media outlet too biased, they can choose a rival. Others argue that there is no real choice. According to them, all media are biased because they serve advertisers, governments and owners or just because they are made the same way, by similar people.

Chile's most popular newspaper, *Las Últimas Noticias* (The Latest News), records which stories visitors read on its website. The popularity of these stories decides what the paper reports the next day.

YES

'Civil libertarians and herbal tea activist types always seem to get upset about the apparent lack of media diversity. What they forget is that when it comes to choosing between objectivity and biased entertainment, audiences vote with their remotes.'

Mike Walsh, founder of Screenmedia, Australia

'Even anti-establishment ideologies - such as those sometimes [expressed] in rap music - will be produced if they meet the test of the market ... products that reflect the values of media owners won't sell unless they serve a market better than their competitors.'

John H. McManus, Market-driven Journalism: Let the Citizen Beware?

'Instead of finding out what its readers wanted and giving it to them, it decided what its readers should want, and thrust it upon them.'

Anon, on the failure of the South China Morning Post, Hong Kong

'I want my journalists to be writing for the people, not for me, or their editors, or the bureaucrats who put out press releases.'

Augustine Edwards, Editor, Las Últimas Noticias, Chile's blog-driven newspaper

✹ STATISTICALLY SPEAKING

• The UK newspaper, *The Independent*, raised daily circulation from 217,000 to 250,000 by changing its shape. Consumers who regularly travel on railways and buses wanted a smaller paper that was easier to handle.

NO

'News organisations must treat information not as a commodity but as a ... right of the citizen. To that end, the media should exploit neither the quality nor the substance of the news or opinions for the purposes of boosting readership or audience figures in order to increase advertising revenue.'

Council of Europe, Resolution 1003; On the ethics of journalism

✘ 'He who prides himself on giving what he thinks the people want is creating a fictitious demand for lower standards, which he will then satisfy.'

Lord Reith, the first chairman of the BBC, 1924

✘ 'If the editor tries to write other than what suits the owner, he is fired the next day. This press, which is the absolutely submissive and characterless slave of the owners, moulds public opinion.'

Adolf Hitler, dictator of Germany, 1940

✿ STATISTICALLY SPEAKING

• A 2001 survey by the *Project for Excellence in Journalism* found that 53% of local news directors 'reported advertisers try to tell them what to air and not to air and they say the problem is growing'.

CASE STUDY

HOWARD STERN

Howard Stern is a radio DJ in the USA known as a 'shock jock' for his outrageous style and explicit programme content. His shows on radio and television during the 1990s brought him fines and controversy as well as a huge public audience. In 2004 Clear Channel, which owns several radio stations, launched a 'self-policing' effort, and declared that there would be no 'indecent' material allowed on the air. This led to the company dismissing several of its own employees, including Stern. He was dropped from six Clear Channel owned stations in Florida, California, Pennsylvania, New York and Kentucky. Many people were concerned that this was against free speech. But, with other radio stations to choose from, audiences still had a choice.

Effect of dropping The Howard Stern Show on local ranking of Clear Channel radio stations

Radio station	Ranking 2003 (with Stern)	Ranking 2004 (after Stern)
WXDX	3rd	11th
WTKS-FM	2nd	8th
WNVE	6th	14th
KIOZ	5th	20th

Source: Arbitron data compiled by Krysten Crawford, CNN

MORE TO THINK ABOUT

If a group in society has its views excluded from the media, what stops it from producing its own media: money, education, the law, apathy?

Q: Does the media influence democratic decisions?

VOTERS COMMITTED to a political idea usually buy a newspaper that shares their goals. But there are many media consumers in most countries who are not committed to one side or another, who may be influenced through the media. Media stories might persuade voters by favouring one side's values, or exposing immoral activity by the other side's politicians.

NO '[When we] tried to investigate the impact of the television coverage of unemployment on [voter beliefs, we] found no convincing evidence of media effects. It seems, rather, that the unemployment coverage was influenced by the public's perceptions of the economy.'

Oliver Quiring, University of Erlangen–Nürnberg, Germany

✗ 'Large media institutions, such as CBS or the *New York Times*, have been regarded as nothing if not authoritative ... authority is a priceless franchise. But it is this franchise that [the media] incredibly, has just thrown away. It did so by choosing to go into overt opposition to one party's candidate, a sitting president. It stooped to conquer.'

Columnist Daniel Henninger on the media's backing of the losing candidate in the USA's 2004 election arguing that media bias had no effect on the election

✱ STATISTICALLY SPEAKING

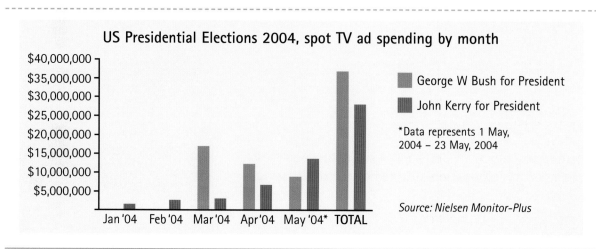

US Presidential Elections 2004, spot TV ad spending by month

- $40,000,000
- $35,000,000
- $30,000,000
- $25,000,000
- $20,000,000
- $15,000,000
- $10,000,000
- $5,000,000

Jan '04   Feb '04   Mar '04   Apr '04   May '04*   TOTAL

■ George W Bush for President
■ John Kerry for President

*Data represents 1 May, 2004 – 23 May, 2004

Source: Nielsen Monitor-Plus

YES

'Murdoch [a media 'mogul'] is the great corrupter of politicians ... Politicians fear they need this bully's patronage. Whenever they cave in, his grip on politics tightens.'

Polly Toynbee, columnist, UK

'In the 1930s, we were afraid that the fascists would take over the government and then control the press: in the twenty-first century, there may be a danger that the fascists will take control of the press and then control the government. The dangers are there.'

Lord McNally of Blackpool, UK

'The Chuan government was brought down after a campaign by [the newspaper] *Thai rat* to expose abuses of a land distribution scheme in Phuket.'

Pasuk & Baker, Political Change in Thailand

'Anyone who believes that the media doesn't affect the way they vote is only fooling themselves. Very few voters obtain all the party manifestos and make decisions based entirely on their contents. All information provided by the media is edited, and therefore biased in some way.'

Jacob Stanley, BBC online Talking Point

Rupert Murdoch, a global media 'mogul', leaves a meeting at No 10 Downing Street, home of the UK's Prime Minister.

MORE TO THINK ABOUT

The media has most power to affect the decisions of people who have no strong views of their own. Those with strong views are more sceptical towards contrary information. Are strong views good for democracy?

11

Q: Does the concentration of media under a few owners need control?

ALL COUNTRIES make rules for media ownership. In 'unfree' countries, such as North Korea, all media may be owned or controlled by the government. In 'free' countries, businesses run the media. But as businesses grow, they buy up their rivals. So there is a risk that all of a community's media could come to be controlled by one business, giving it control of all the information available to people. This could have an effect on viewpoints from politics to advertising. How are democracies best protected from such risks?

❖ STATISTICALLY SPEAKING

• Just after World War II, four out of five US newspapers were independently owned. By 1989, only one in five was independent.

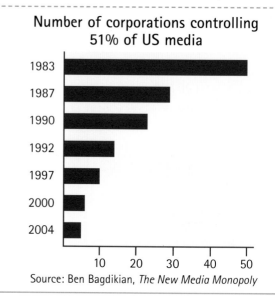

Number of corporations controlling 51% of US media

Source: Ben Bagdikian, *The New Media Monopoly*

YES 'I think it is absolutely essential in a democracy to have competition in the media, a lot of competition, and we seem to be moving away from that.'
Walter Cronkite, former CBS News anchorman

✓ 'Radio consolidation has contributed to a 34% decline in the number of owners, a 90% rise in the cost of advertising rates, [and] a rise in indecent broadcasts. If ever there were a cautionary tale, this is it.'
Senator Hollings, South Carolina, USA, on loosened controls on radio ownership

✓ 'There is a danger that France will follow Italy into conditions that are dangerous for democracy – when media power is concentrated in the hands of a powerful few.'
Aidan White, European Federation of Journalists, 2004

❖ STATISTICALLY SPEAKING

• Socpresse and Lagardère, two corporations based on weapons manufacture, own between them over 70% of the French press.

CASE STUDY

US RADIO

Lowry Mays acted fast when the US government loosened controls on ownership of radio stations. Before 1996, the limit was 40 stations. Mays' Clear Channel soon controlled 1,200 – around 50% of US radio. In 2003, two million Americans protested against a change to ownership rules made by the US media regulator. The new rules would permit one company, such as Clear Channel, to own up to 45% of a community's media. Legal action finally stopped the new rules coming into force in 2005.

Protestors against new ownership rules picket a Clear Channel radio station in California.

NO 'Common ownership can actually increase content diversity. The reason is simple – while owners with only one outlet each may all compete for a lowest-common-denominator market, owners with several outlets each are able to target niche markets with different programming on each station.'

James Gattuso, The Myth of Media Concentration

✗ 'Covering the Iraq invasion, a Canadian media giant "used a lot of the print reporters on the television reports. Their coverage, on television in particular, was much enhanced by [access] to the print people".'

Professor Donna Logan, giving evidence to Canadian senators

✗ 'It is essential that the UK reinforces its position as one of the most attractive places for communications companies to do business. Unnecessary regulations need to be removed wherever possible. By eliminating undue burdens on business we can drive innovation, increase investment, raise employment and bring better services to consumers.'

UK government's introduction to a Communications Bill

MORE TO THINK ABOUT

It is hard to let powerful people act freely, while protecting the freedoms of less powerful people. If you owned a newspaper, would you think it was fair for the government to ban you from buying a TV station?

Q: Should public benefit come before profit?

COMMERCIAL MEDIA have two goals. Their first goal is to survive in a competitive marketplace, by earning more than they spend. Their second goal is to provide high quality information, of benefit to the public. But high quality information is expensive to research, and may sometimes conflict with a media business's partners, such as advertisers.

NO 'Our jobs as leaders of newspaper enterprises is to find the sweet spot where we can fulfill both our [profit] obligation to the shareholders and our social obligation to provide communities with the kind of information they need in order for people to make their sovereign choices wisely.'
Jack Fuller, head of the US Tribune Company

✗ 'We're not in the business of providing news and information. We're not in the business of providing well-researched music. We're simply in the business of selling our customers' products.'
Lowry Mays, CEO of US radio corporation Clear Channel

✗ 'A director must recognise that the primary responsibility is to the Company's shareholders as a whole but should, where appropriate, have regard for the interests of all stakeholders of the Company.'
Code of Conduct for Directors, West Australian Newspapers Holdings Ltd

CASE STUDY

JAY HARRIS

Jay Harris resigned from the San Jose *Mercury News* when its owners, Knight Ridder, decided to improve profits by cutting staff in the newsroom. Harris said, 'When the interest of readers and shareholders are at odds, which takes priority? When the interest of a community and shareholders are at odds, which takes priority? When the interest of the nation and an informed citizenry and the demands of shareholders' forever increasing profits are at odds, which takes priority?'. He launched The Center for the Study of Journalism and Democracy at the University of Southern California, USA.

YES

'Many traditional media are maintaining their profitability by focusing on costs, including cutting back in their newsrooms. Our study shows general increases in journalist workload, declines in numbers of reporters, shrinking space in newscasts to make more room for [adverts] and promotions, and in various ways that are measurable, thinning the product.'

www.stateofthenewsmedia.org Annual Report stating concern that profit-driven media outlets reduce the public benefit of the product

✔ 'We now, with very few exceptions, have an industry run by managers with the mentality of 18th and 19th century mill owners, where workers are costs, not assets, where slashing overheads is more important than nurturing talent, where fear and loathing are poisoning creativity.'

Tony Garnett, speech to the Drama Forum, London

✔ 'The tendency to give the public what it allegedly wants – meaning what is profitable – over what is obviously in the interest of the public understanding, has undermined national security.'

Lowell Bergman, public service journalist (PBS)

✱ STATISTICALLY SPEAKING

• This Japanese survey found that newspapers in Japan earn more from their readers than from their advertisers. How might this affect the newspaper's priorities?

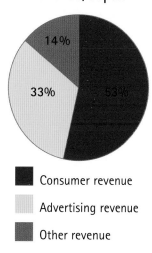

Percentage share of newspaper revenue, Japan

- 14%
- 33%
- 53%

■ Consumer revenue

▫ Advertising revenue

■ Other revenue

Source: Survey by Nihon Shinbun Kyokai

MORE TO THINK ABOUT

Not all media are privately owned. Some media are run by independent trusts (such as charities), or state owned. Which would you expect to be the best source of information?

FIND OUT MORE: www.democraticmedia.org www.freepress.net www.wpfc.org www.pressnet.or.jp/english

Q: Is advertising to children wrong?

SWEDEN BANS advertising on its children's TV stations, to the extent that theme tunes such as the Pokemon song (with the words 'Gotta catch 'em all') are censored if they are likely to encourage children to buy a product. Ireland, Greece, Italy, Denmark and parts of Belgium and Canada all impose restrictions, and other countries are considering a ban. In 2004, a group of doctors in Australia described advertising to children as child abuse.

In 2003, health critics complained about Coca-Cola adverts on the sides of canned drink dispensers in Scottish schools. Coca-Cola replaced its adverts with pictures of children playing, agreeing that schools should be 'commercial-free'.

YES

'Children – and in particular, young children from the age of 12 downwards – are not sufficiently developed intellectually to cope with the full, unrestricted force of advertising.'
Senator Feargal Quinn, Ireland

'There is clear conflict of interest between public health goals of encouraging healthy eating and good eating habits in childhood, and the commercial interests of advertisers seeking to advertise food of low nutritional value to children.'
Sue Kedgley, MP, New Zealand

'Children who watch a lot of television want more toys seen in advertisements and eat more advertised food than children who do not watch as much television.'
Strasburger & Wilson, Children, adolescents and the media

'Those beliefs get burned into those children's brains at an emotional level ... it controls their behaviour for the rest of their life.'
Doctor Michael McDowell, Royal Australasian College of Physicians

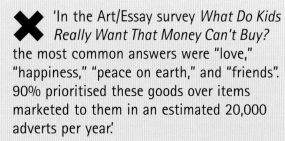

NO 'Advertising should not be looked at like some villain, because it can be used as a source for good. We are never going to solve this [obesity] problem by trying to ban things.'

Jeremy Preston, director of the UK-based Food Advertising Unit

CONFLICTING EVIDENCE?

Sweden has banned TV advertising to under-12s since 1991 and the Flemish part of Belgium bans ads within five minutes of programmes aimed at children. Quebec, Canada has had a ban for many years. 'There is no factual evidence that a ban will eliminate or reduce obesity ... Where this has happened in Sweden and Canada it has made no difference.'

Jeremy Preston, director of the UK-based Food Advertising Unit

✖ 'In the Art/Essay survey *What Do Kids Really Want That Money Can't Buy?* the most common answers were "love," "happiness," "peace on earth," and "friends". 90% prioritised these goods over items marketed to them in an estimated 20,000 adverts per year.'

Widmeyer Communications survey, USA

✖ 'Kraft [the food company] is doing parents a real favour by recognising that foods of poor nutritional quality should not be advertised to kids. By setting nutrition standards for foods advertised to 6–11-year-olds, Kraft will make it a little easier to reduce kids' consumption of foods high in calories, saturated and trans fat, or added sugars.'

Margo G. Wootan, Center for Science in the Public Interest

How far do parents feel their children's diets are influenced by adverts?

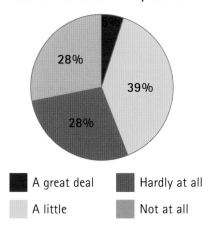

5%
28%
39%
28%

■ A great deal   ■ Hardly at all
■ A little   ■ Not at all

Source: Yougov.com poll, UK

MORE TO THINK ABOUT

Advertisers design their TV adverts to appeal to those viewers who they think will be watching when their advert is shown. Try watching adverts on a programme or channel you think is boring. See if you can tell what sort of viewer the advertiser is aiming at there.

Does it matter if children are influenced by adverts when they don't themselves have a lot of financial power? How much do you think they can influence their parents?

Q: Should the media report on the private lives of public figures?

CELEBRITIES SOMETIMES try to stop media intrusion into their private lives. Most celebrities employ experts, called 'PRs', who control which media are allowed to interview, film and report on their client. Sometimes celebrities go to court to stop a newspaper or news programme from revealing something personal. But the law finds it hard to strike a balance between protecting their right to privacy, and ensuring other public figures, such as politicians, cannot escape public scrutiny.

CASE STUDY

PRINCESS CAROLINE
In 2004, Princess Caroline of Monaco won a case forcing EU media to respect her right to privacy in public spaces. Three German magazines had published pictures of her doing her shopping.

❉ STATISTICALLY SPEAKING

• 'Statistics from the NSW Privacy Commissioner indicate that only 1.6% of complaints received by his office arise from intrusions by the media.'
NSW Law Reform Commission, Australia

YES

'Celebrities such as Hollywood star George Clooney complain about video stalkers and the paparazzi engaging in a "malicious free for all" to report their private lives, but reveal details about their private lives in magazine interviews. Objections are not made to privacy intrusion [itself]. Rather, it seems that claiming "privacy intrusion" is one of the most effective ways for certain individuals to control unwanted publicity and stop investigations into their lives.'
Tessa Mayes, Restraint or Revelation? www.spiked-online.com report

'Take away the right to investigate the drug habits of a children's TV presenter or the sex antics of an apparently upstanding and happily married police chief – role models all in their public personas – and you also take away the right to investigate [a long list of corrupt politicians].'
Neil Wallis, editor of The People newspaper, UK

'Despite all the complaints from celebrities about being stalked by the paparazzi, their publicists actually enter into deals with the celebrity tabloids to make sure their stars get exposure. It's an odd relationship that benefits both sides.'
ABC Newstore, USA

NO 'The idea that because you deny something about your private life automatically entitles the media to publish otherwise private information seems to me to be very harsh indeed and doesn't seem to recognise that there may be all sorts of conditions that someone should want to keep private.'

Naomi Campbell, model and litigant against The Mirror newspaper, UK

✖ 'The press is sometimes its own worst enemy with its over-concentration on trivia.'

Lord Mostyn, House of Lords, UK

✖ 'People think because you're famous they have the right to know everything about you, and I don't think that's true.'

Publicist Cari Ross, who handles US actresses Jennifer Connelly and Salma Hayek

These photographers – sometimes called 'paparazzi' – earn a living taking photos of celebrities. Consumers enjoy glimpses of celebrities' private lives. So newspapers pay well for photos which expose a celebrity's private moments.

MORE TO THINK ABOUT
Are you sympathetic to a celebrity who hates being 'hunted' by the media? Are you fascinated by 'inside information' about their lives? Which of these conflicting interests matters most to you? Should celebrities who 'court' the media to gain publicity and improve their careers be prepared to accept intrusive consequences?

FIND OUT MORE: www.informationcommissioner.gov.uk www.bbc.co.uk/celebdaq www.privacyinternational.org www.ukeditors.com

Q: Should journalists be allowed to keep sources 'off the record'?

JOURNALISTS NEED good sources to be able to inform us well. But some 'whistleblowers' will only give information to a journalist in exchange for a promise to keep their role secret. However, this means that it's more difficult for consumers to decide what they believe when they don't know who was the source.

CASE STUDY 1

THE HILLSBOROUGH DISASTER

On 15th April 1989, 96 football fans lost their lives at a football match because of overcrowding in the central standing area allocated to fans of Liverpool Football Club.

Liverpudlians demanded that UK tabloid *The Sun* identify its source after the newspaper published information from secret police sources who blamed the Hillsborough football stadium tragedy on Liverpool fans. *The Sun* lost 95% of its 200,000 readers in Liverpool. An inquiry later found the police themselves were at fault.

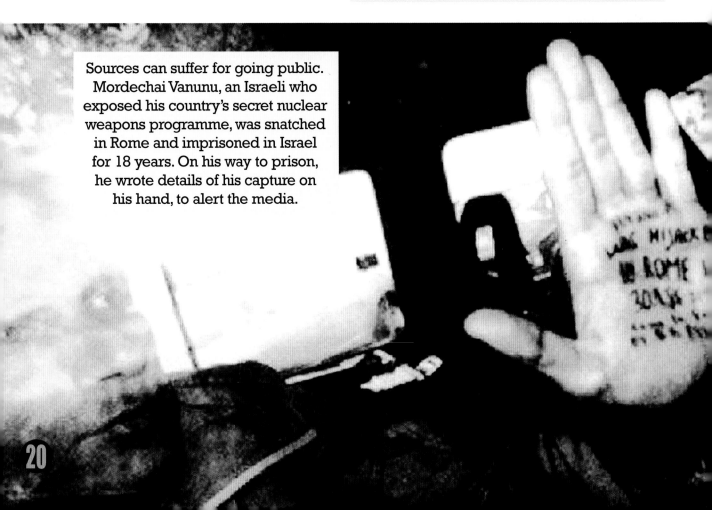

Sources can suffer for going public. Mordechai Vanunu, an Israeli who exposed his country's secret nuclear weapons programme, was snatched in Rome and imprisoned in Israel for 18 years. On his way to prison, he wrote details of his capture on his hand, to alert the media.

YES

'The contract between a reporter and an unnamed source – the offer of information in return for anonymity – is properly a binding one. But I believe that a source who turns out to have lied has breached that contract, and can fairly be exposed.'

Daniel Okrent, New York Times Ombudsman

✓ 'I'm not so sure any more that Burma is worse than Brussels.'

Hans-Martin Tillack of Germany's Stern magazine criticises press freedom in Belgium, after being raided by Belgian police hunting his source for secret EU memos

✓ 'The BBC and Andrew Gilligan were right to refuse to disclose David Kelly's identity to the government or the public – in contrast to the government, which sought to manoeuvre Dr Kelly's name into the public domain, without appearing to be responsible.'

The National Union of Journalists UK, after the suicide of Dr David Kelly, a source whose identity was revealed

NO

'The widespread failure to attribute facts and quotations has become a cancer eating away at the ethical standards of news reporting ... it is not uncommon for the main stories leading the front page [of *The Times*, London] to be based entirely on anonymous sources ... thirty years ago it was rare indeed.'

Nicholas Jones, Sultans of Spin

✗ 'People judge communication by its source so when you deny people full knowledge of that source of information they are losing something important about evaluating the message.'

Kathleen Hall Jamison, Annenberg School for Communication, University of Southern California, USA

✗ 'Anonymity allows the media to be used. It robs readers of any way to judge the source. It lets people speak without taking responsibility. It undermines [the media's] credibility. Yet it is common practice among our most revered journalists.'

Geneva Overholser, journalist and academic

CASE STUDY 2

FINDING A SOURCE

In 1995 a Queensland court tried to reveal the identity of a journalist's source in an Australian political scandal, without the journalist's cooperation. It proved to be very difficult:

Days spent: 27
Witnesses heard: 48
Items entered into evidence: 272
Expense: over A$1m
Sources identified: none

MORE TO THINK ABOUT

Journalists often have to defy a court's order instructing them to confess their source. Some journalists' unions help journalists to hide their files. Do you think it is right to act 'illegally' in these cases?

Q: Is TV to blame for changes in the way families socialise?

A GENERATION AGO, children typically watched an hour or so of television before an evening meal, and two or three hours on a Saturday morning. By 2005, children were more likely to eat their evening meal in front of the television, and many had a TV in their own room. Solitary television watching, as opposed to 'family viewing', is on the rise. These changes might be caused by television, or result from other pressures on the family.

Interviewer: So what makes [the news] a grown-ups' programme?

(Six-year-old A): It's boring.

Interviewer: So does that mean that grown-ups are boring?

(Six-year-old B): Yes, because they like the news.

(Six-year-old A): I hate the news.

Interviewer: Why do you think grown-ups like the news?

(Six-year-old A): Because they want to know what's happening?

Interviewer: And aren't you interested?

(Six-year-old A): No!

Source: Buckingham et al

More children have a television in their bedroom than ever before. Experts disagree over the possible consequences of this.

YES

'The [idea] that the sole responsibility lies with parents is a self-justifying claim usually made by people who wish to evade accountability. It is much like pumping sewage into a town's river, while maintaining that parents are responsible for protecting the health of their own children.'

Parents' Television Council website

'One important ... study of the introduction of television in three Canadian towns found the same pattern ... across time. A major effect of television's arrival was the reduction in participation in social, recreational, and community activities among people of all ages. In short, television privatises our leisure time.'

Robert Putnam, The strange disappearance of Civic America

CONFLICTING EVIDENCE?

'25% of American children younger than two have a television in their bedroom.'

Source: www.kff.org, Zero to Six

---------------------⬇---------------------

According to the child trends data bank, the average number of hours watched per American child fell in the period 1990-2005 by around 5%.

NO

Are other social factors to blame? 'Married-couple households have declined from 80% in the '50s to just 51% today. Meanwhile, the number of singles 18-plus has surged to 86 million. In 2000, for the first time, households with people living alone outnumbered households with couples and children, 26% to 24%, the latter figure down sharply from 1970s 40%.'

Michael Tchong, The New Family Ecosystem

✖ 'Lengthy, time-consuming commuting takes away from potential time spent with family, friends and community ... The trend from 1986-98 varies, but is towards increased commuting time.'
Jackson et al, Canada

✖ 'Parents who talk to their children about television programmes more often are also more likely to report having seen media have a positive effect on their children. Parents who report that their children "always" or "often" watch educational television are less likely to report having seen media have a negative effect on their children.'
National Survey of Family Media Habits, USA

✸ STATISTICALLY SPEAKING

• In 1900, 5% of mothers of children under the age of 16 were in full-time or part-time work. In 2000, the proportion was 65%.

MORE TO THINK ABOUT

Are you missing out on friends and fun when you watch television? Or do you need to watch TV to share cultural experience with your friends?

FIND OUT MORE: www.parentstv.org www.kff.org
www.childtrendsdatabank.org www.limitv.org

Q: Do media images of models harm our self-esteem?

WOMEN'S AND girls' media and advertising usually only show photographs of thin women. Consumers appear not to want to buy pictures of women who look normal. Instead, they prefer to see models who seem more glamorous than them. This is known as 'aspirational' consumption, since the consumer 'aspires' to look more glamorous. Some girls and young women may become depressed that they look less glamorous, not realising that (for example) photographs may be manipulated to make models look even thinner.

YES

'Nobody was dieting in Fiji ten years ago [before TV was available]. The teenagers see TV as a model for how one gets by in the modern world. They believe the shows depict reality.'

Anne Becker, Harvard Medical School, USA

'Perhaps I am deluded in thinking that my jowls are an advertisement for courage, proclaiming that I'm not afraid of growing old. Maybe they are shrieking that I am a clueless loser who doesn't have the wherewithal to have my chin taken care of.'

Mary Tannen, Beauty Editor, New York Times, USA

'The media is obsessed with being young.'

Dr Allan Kaplan, eating disorders expert at Toronto General Hospital, Canada

CASE STUDY

A 'NORMAL' MODEL

In the late 1990s, readers and advertisers asked magazines to use women with more natural figures. The model Sophie Dahl was a size 14 when she was 'discovered' by Isabella Blow, a New York fashion guru. Despite a good reception to this innovation, extremely thin models have remained the 'norm' in the industry.

STATISTICALLY SPEAKING

- Four out of ten UK girls aged 14–15 skip breakfast.
- In 1998 [after the arrival of US TV], 74% of Fijian teenage girls reported feeling 'too big or fat'.

NO

'There is a larger dynamic behind cultural trends, which drive behaviours, cultural values and attitudes. [Changing media images] would be swimming against the tide ... The media is sensitive to [fashion] trends and brings them to the surface. In this respect they are seen to be trend creators, yet they are just mirrors of patterns which already exist.'

Deanne Jade, National Centre for Eating Disorders, UK

'The story of Cinderella, of Chinese origin, highlights the importance of such myths in traditional society ... In the myth, the desirability of a woman is judged by the size of her foot. Should it be too big, the consequence is complete rejection.'

Patricia Karetzky, curator of Femininity exhibition, Lehman College Gallery, New York, USA

'No child needs to be told fat is bad when right from nursery school it's the fat kids that get tormented for being slow, ugly and undesirable – often reinforced by teachers who see them as losers, too. From *Charlie and the Chocolate Factory* to *Harry Potter*, heroes are skinny and lithe, while nasty children are fat porkers.'

Polly Toynbee, columnist

✳ STATISTICALLY SPEAKING

• Nearly half of all girls aged 7–16 read a girls' magazine each week.

MORE TO THINK ABOUT

This debate investigated whether the media causes a person to dislike their body. Is the media the only cause, the main cause, among the causes, or just holding up a 'mirror' to a real, social cause?

Most teenagers work hard to find a self-image they are comfortable with. How much are media messages absorbed by teenagers?

FIND OUT MORE: www.everybody.co.nz www.eating-disorders.org.uk
www.anorexia.org http://edr.org.uk

Q: Does access to government files improve democracy?

MANY GOVERNMENT decisions are kept secret from the public. Some secrets are necessary for national security or the health of the economy. But governments can use that explanation to hide information that could embarrass them. Media and democracy campaigners no longer trust governments to be fully honest. So they demand tougher Freedom of Information (FOI) laws, to force politicians to release information.

YES

'Freedom of information is a fundamental tool for media to ensure the public interest is served.'
Anne Kothawala, President and CEO, Canadian Newspaper Association

'The culture of secrecy that has been the [habit] of governments for centuries is no longer feasible in a global age of information. Governments ... must provide information to succeed.'
David Banisar, The FreedomInfo.Org Survey

'Secrecy allows inefficiency, wastefulness and corruption to thrive.'
Mukelani Dimba, Open Democracy Advice Centre

CASE STUDY

BSE AND A COVER-UP

In 1986 a disease called BSE or 'mad cow disease' was first identified in cattle in the UK. Ten years later it was revealed that the disease could possibly be passed to humans. A new type of brain disease, vCJD, is widely believed to result from eating BSE-infected beef. A special inquiry was set up in 1998 to investigate the scandal. The report concluded:

'The Government did not lie to the public about BSE ... [it] was preoccupied with preventing an alarmist over-reaction to BSE because it believed that the risk was remote. It is now clear that this campaign of reassurance was a mistake. When ... the Government announced that BSE had probably been transmitted to humans, the public felt that they had been betrayed. Confidence in government pronouncements about risk was a further casualty of BSE.'

The body of a BSE-infected cow.

Selection of FOI schemes currently in operation

Country	Since	Ease of access	Access on appeal	Problems
Australia	1982	Good	At risk	No independent referee, budget cuts
Belgium	1994	Good	Good	Vague rules permit secrecy
Canada	1983	Fair	Excellent	Attempts to restore secrecy, well resisted
Czech Republic	2000	Fair	Expensive	Vague rules permit secrecy
Denmark	1970	Good	Poor	Currently under review
France	1978	Good	Fair	Independent referee's orders not compulsory
Iceland	1996	Good	Good	Several types of information exempted
India	–	–	–	Some states have passed local FOI laws
Ireland	1998	Fair	Expensive	Government moves to restore secrecy, 2003–4
Japan	2001	Good	Good	Ministries (eg Defence) illegally hiding info
Netherlands	1978	Good	Fair	Security information secret for 75 years
New Zealand	1982	Good	Good	Poor accountability, one scandal: 'Corngate'
Norway	1970	Good	Fair	Ministers suspected of illegally hiding info
Panama	2002	Fair	Poor	Enquirers must prove 'legal interest' in info
Spain	1992	Good	Fair	Some vague rules permit secrecy
Sweden	1766	Good	Good	Full awareness and use of the law is lacking
Turkey	2004	tba-	tba-	Too new to assess
UK	2005	tba-	tba-	Voluntary 'code' abused by ministers in 2001
USA	1967	Slow	At risk	Moves to restore secrecy, 2001–2004

Summarised from The FreedomInfo.Org Global Survey, May 2004

NO 'Most of the key discussions take place in informal meetings in Tony Blair's den before cabinet. All the important decisions on the Iraq war were taken in this way; cabinet merely rubber-stamped them. So even if the papers were released, they wouldn't tell us very much because they would be so bland as to be virtually worthless.'

Anthony Seldon, biographer of Tony Blair, Prime Minister, UK

✗ '[In 1974] President Ford vetoed the Freedom of Information Act ... because he and Rumsfeld and Cheney believed that it took away too much presidential power. It allowed courts to order the release of documents even when the president said they shouldn't be released.'

Thomas Blanton, National Security Archive (USA), interviewed by Bill Moyers

MORE TO THINK ABOUT

If governments are forced to make their records available to the public, will politicians and public officials stop using email, and talk instead? How might FOI laws force politicians to act more openly?

Q: Is the media responsible for 'personality' politics?

POLITICAL ISSUES to do with the economy, national security, or healthcare, are complex. Complex issues are harder to turn into exciting television or gripping reading in a newspaper. But people are fascinated by personal stories – of power struggles, bravery, betrayals... So politicians and media both might prefer to present politics as a battle of personalities. This poses risks for democracy. Personality cults are typical of authoritarian regimes.

US Presidential elections feature televised debates between the leading candidates (on the left is John Kerry, right George W Bush). Media coverage of these debates often comments on character and style, with less attention to political argument.

YES

'Because of television, the power of these leaders is essentially personal. Voters support them, not their party or ideology. These leaders don't need a party or ideology. They have television. Television allows direct, personal communication between politicians and voters.'

William Schneider, Personality Politics conquers Japan, in The Atlantic

'Television loves sagas in which someone wins and someone loses. It abhors long, tedious, complex stories and will usually ignore them if possible.'

David Gergen, Professor of Public Service, Harvard, USA

✵ STATISTICALLY SPEAKING

• In the 2004 US Presidential election, 44% of news stories which claimed a character trait (eg honesty, arrogance) for a candidate offered no supporting evidence for the claim. The most frequently unsupported character trait was Bush's decisiveness – 57% of such claims lacked evidence.

✳ STATISTICALLY SPEAKING

• The personality of the 2004 Democrat Presidential candidate, John Kerry, was treated differently by the media in 2000, when he was a possible running-mate for the previous Democrat candidate, Al Gore:

Media outlet	2000 description of Kerry's personality	2004 description of Kerry's personality
St Petersburg Times	'Easy manner', 'good looks', 'would bring some charm to the ticket'	'rarely do [Democrats] have much to say about [his] personal appeal or charisma'
NBC News / Hardball	Choosing Kerry would signal that Gore 'thinks the election will be decided on personality'.	'nobody ever associated the word charisma with [Kerry]'
Boston Globe	'Younger and more telegenic than Dick Cheney'	'He has thus far demonstrated all the charisma of a cold roast beef sandwich'
Daily News (NY)	'a [military] record tailor-made to undermine the standard Republican attack on liberal Democrats'	'charisma-challenged by a mannequin'

NO 'Party membership remains pitifully small and party organisations weak. Decisions are typically made by a small centralised clique, and party organisation tends to be ... isolated from society and the influence of rank-and-file members ... As a result, personality politics have assumed a central role in Latvian political life.'
Daunis Auers, Latvia's 2002 elections

✖ Explaining why family name – Kennedy, Bush – matters: 'People somehow think subconsciously that this family has been tested ... To them, that name connotes quality.'
Henry Graff, historian (USA)

✖ '[In Armenia's 1999 election], the parties have pursued the strategy of personality politics – relying on the opinion of voters of the character and legitimacy of their major members.'
The European Institute For The Media

CASE STUDY

IT'S ALL LOOKS?
Researchers at University College, Cork (Ireland) studied the effect of ballot paper photographs in local and European elections. Using actual ballot photographs from a Dublin electoral area, voters were asked to rank candidates in order of their preference. Survey responses matched actual electoral outcomes in four out of five cases. Results included:
• Young female candidates performed best.
• Female voters display a preference for young, attractive male candidates.
• The oldest-looking candidate on the ballot paper ranked lowest.

MORE TO THINK ABOUT
If politicians use 'soap opera' to appeal to voters, does this mean that voters are to blame? Is it wrong for voters to rely on their 'feelings' about an individual politician? Should the media try to prevent voters from doing so?

Q: Should the media hire more journalists of different classes, genders or cultures?

APART FROM 'editorials' most journalistic articles and news programmes try to be as neutral as possible. But some types of personal experience are hard to communicate across cultural divides. A black journalist with personal experience of racism will have a better idea of how many black readers feel about a story that involves racism. A white journalist may lack that sensitivity. However, actively having policies of 'positive discrimination' may lead to less qualified people gaining a job over more qualified. Furthermore can positive discrimination really end bias anyway?

YES

'We advocate for fair, representative, accurate journalism, by changing the complexion of newsrooms, not just racially and ethnically, but through the natural diversity of thought that occurs when you bring in people with different backgrounds.'

Ernest Sotomayor, President of Unity, a US minority journalists' organisation

'Many important decisions in the media are being made by arrogant, young, underexposed writers and producers. Too often they fall back on stereotypes for characters.'

Dennis Greene, Professor of Law, University of Oregon, USA

❂ STATISTICALLY SPEAKING

The annual Knight Foundation survey of American newspapers compares the percentage of ethnic minority staff to the percentage of ethnic minority citizens in the area each newspaper serves:

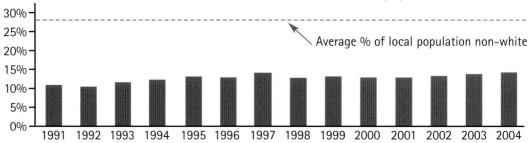

Average % of local population non-white

The Dutch Association of Journalists (NVJ) set up a course, Islam for Journalists, in October 2001. The course helps non-Muslim journalists understand Islamic issues, to cover them more sensitively.

✳ STATISTICALLY SPEAKING

• In a survey of journalists in Australia it was found that the fathers (or main bread-winning parents) of 61% of the journalists had white-collar occupations – most of these in professional or managerial jobs. By contrast, in the national workforce as a whole, 21% of people are in professional or managerial occupations. Fewer than 3 out of 10 journalists are from blue-collar homes, while one in 10 had parents in primary industry.

NO 'The good news about diversity is that it has opened the doors to a lot of talented minority journalists who may have had a hard time in the past getting in. The bad news, however, is it's also opened up the doors to political correctness, racial and ethnic hypersensitivity and group favouritism that undercuts the candour and the completeness and accuracy of the news, on a lot of controversial subjects, particularly, affirmative action, immigration, race and gay rights.'

William McGowan, Colouring the News: How Crusading for Diversity has Corrupted American Journalism

MORE TO THINK ABOUT

Some media recruiters say that they cannot find enough qualified applicants among minority and disadvantaged groups. Do you think the media has a duty to provide that education, or should public education be improved?

Q: Should the media censor extremists' views?

THE MEDIA have to decide how to present the views of extreme political or religious groups, especially during elections. In some countries, laws ban such groups from public speech. But in most democratic countries, private media businesses set their own rules, guided by what they think their consumers would want. Banning a group lets it win sympathy for being 'oppressed'. But reporting its views might seem to make those views respectable.

YES

'Terrorists use sensationalism to vastly amplify their message. They know that horror and drama capture the media's attention, so they manufacture them. This is why instead of merely executing their victims, [hostage takers in Iraq] cut off their heads on camera and broadcast the videos. When that gets old, which it will, they will come up with something even more awful.'

Mark Bowden, The Atlantic magazine

Democratic nations 'must try to find ways to starve the terrorist and the hijacker of the oxygen of publicity on which they depend.'

Margaret Thatcher, then UK Prime Minister

✿ STATISTICALLY SPEAKING

• In a survey of 107 male and 123 female college students on the perceived harm of hate speech and the importance of freedom of speech, women were more negative regarding the harm of hate speech and regarded freedom of speech as less important than men.

The British National Party (BNP), a 'white rights' group linked with racist violence, is often banned from stating its extreme claims. It gains publicity from the free speech debate that follows. Here BNP candidate Nick Griffin salutes wearing a gag over his mouth, after all candidates in an election area were banned from making speeches.

GAGGED FOR

NO

'Congress shall make no law respecting an establishment of religion, or prohibiting the free exercise thereof; or abridging the freedom of speech, or of the press; or the right of the people peaceably to assemble, and to petition the government for a redress of grievances.'

US Bill of Rights, First amendment

✖ 'We say that the media affects some of the people some of the time in some contexts. The media is crucial in setting the agenda – in telling us what to focus on – but people don't accept what the media says lock, stock and barrel. The research shows they are more discriminating than that.'

Laura Leets, Professor of Communication, Stanford University, USA

✖ 'As somebody who has been involved for years in defending legal abortion by trying to promote a rational public understanding of the issues involved, I am happy to allow my opponents to expose themselves for what they are – dishonest, manipulative, irrational, ignorant fanatics who patronise women ...'

Ann Furedi, bpas (a pregnancy advisory service), criticising a BBC ban on an anti-abortion election advert

✖ 'To suppress [hate speech] is not to resolve the hatred but perhaps to drive it underground and thereby encourage acts of violence ... Any restrictions on expression should be justified only by reference to its impact such as the likelihood of ... imminent lawless action.'

Council of Europe

CASE STUDY

WEBSITE CLOSURES

500 Arabic-language websites were taken off-line in September 2001, by a massive raid by US law enforcement officials on InfoCom, a Texas-based company. The raid occurred six days before the largest terror attack in US history.

✸ STATISTICALLY SPEAKING

• With a global Internet, individual countries may find it difficult to censor something completely, only drive it 'underground'. As the chart shows, if something is not available in one country people may be able to find it through another.

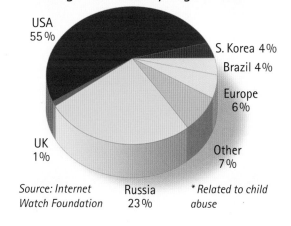

Illegal* Content by Region 2003

USA 55%
S. Korea 4%
Brazil 4%
Europe 6%
Other 7%
Russia 23%
UK 1%

Source: Internet Watch Foundation

* Related to child abuse

MORE TO THINK ABOUT

Disagreements often lead to people feeling offended. Extreme political opinions are likely to cause the most offence. But how can a society decide which speech is too extreme, and which should be protected under the right to free speech?

Q: Does violence on screen affect the morals of viewers?

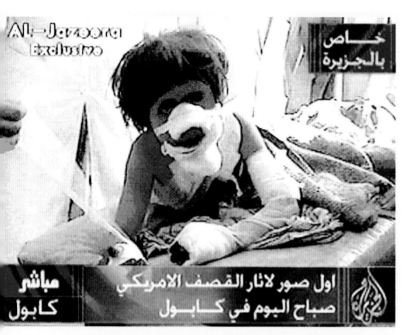

Al-Jazeera Exclusive

خاص بالجزيرة

اول صور لاثار القصف الامريكي
صباح اليوم في كـابول

مباشر
كابول

TV violence is mainly seen in films and dramas. News about real violence, such as war, is censored to remove upsetting images. The Al-Jazeera news channel was criticised for showing the real effects of violence in the 2003 invasion of Iraq.

As THE cultural gap between teenagers and adults grew wider in the 1960s and 1970s, many adults blamed violent TV programmes for rising crime. An investigation by US politicians in 1982 raised many questions. Research shows that children who watch a lot of television are about 10% more likely to be isolated, fearful and depressed, and perhaps violent. But is this due to TV itself, or did they watch extra TV because of other, more important factors, such as social exclusion?

YES 'Violence on television encourages people to grow up thinking that violence is an acceptable way of operating.'
Charles Clarke, then UK Education Minister

'Inevitably, if you go on seeing sex and violence year after year, you get habituated to it.'
James Ferman, former Director of UK censor BBFC

'Most heavy viewers in every education, age, income, sex, newspaper reading and neighbourhood category express a greater sense of insecurity and apprehension than do light viewers ... Fearful people are most dependent, more easily manipulated and controlled ... They may accept and even welcome repression [stronger government laws] if it promises to relieve their insecurities. That is the deeper problem of violence-laden television.'
George Gerbner, Annenberg School of Communications, USA

NO

'With this single focus we ignore many of the root causes of societal ills.'

Gene Mater, CBS, testimony to a congressional hearing, USA

❌ 'Probably the chief stumbling block to reaching any definitive conclusions is that almost everyone has a television set .... The crucial controlled experiment – comparing individuals who have television with those who do not – cannot be done.'

Howard Gardner, psychology and child development expert

CONFLICTING EVIDENCE?

'[TV] may play a significant role in shaping behavioural style, when and how violence, aggressiveness or other antisocial behaviour gets expressed.'

David Pearl, National Institute of Mental Health (NIMH), USA

-------------------- ⬇ --------------------

'There's some understandable confusion about [the NIMH research]. It was highly publicised as comprehensive, but it was in fact very narrowly based ... And while it concluded that viewing television violence causes aggressiveness, it did not find a single study which confirmed that television violence causes behaviour that could be characterised as violent in any socially significant way.'

Gene Jankowski, President, CBS Broadcast Group, USA

✱ STATISTICALLY SPEAKING

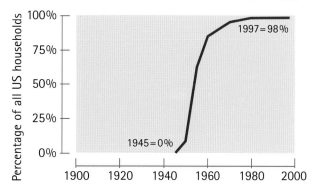

Households with at least one television set

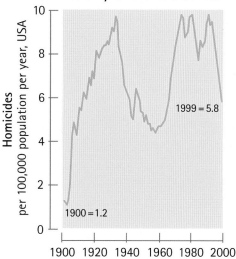

Century of violent crimes

MORE TO THINK ABOUT

When someone tells us a story that troubles us, there is a saying, 'Don't shoot the messenger', which reminds us not to blame the messenger for bad news. Is TV simply a messenger for modern culture's messages, good and bad? Or do you think it always distorts the message?

Q: Do films need censoring?

ANY MEDIUM which can 'overwhelm' its audience can be suspected of having too much power. In the ancient Greek world, thinkers called for a ban on poetry, with its fantastic tales of bravery and violence. Socrates opposed the alphabet, arguing that the written word destroyed our talent for remembering. Newspapers, theatres, colour adverts and TV were each accused. Cinema films, computer games and the Internet are the latest examples in that long debate.

Battle Royale is a Japanese film about 15-year-old school students taking part in a *Survivor*-type competition, but with guns. The film received a Restricted-15 rating from Japan's Film Ethics Committee. The film's makers objected, but withdrew their objection when politicians threatened to censor the film even more heavily.

YES

'We all have the ability to make a choice. Most readers are more than capable of exercising that choice. Reading requires effort and the exercise of imagination, in a way that watching a film does not. That's why I do believe that films should be censored, but not novels.'
Natasha Cooper, crime novelist

'State security is jeopardised and public order is endangered if this film is shown.'
India's film censor, banning Final Solution, a documentary film about religious riots in Gujarat

'Film is a very influential medium and students of the art will readily acknowledge how the cinema has played a crucial role in shaping the values that prevail in any society. The cinema has always been [the leader] of social change and the most cunning achievement of film producers and programme makers has been to convince everyone that any attempt to constrain their "freedom of expression" is "censorship".'
John Beyer, Corrupting Public Morals, in the Catholic Herald

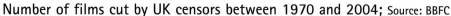

NO 'Some 12,500 [people] have seen the film and there has been not one complaint made. [Film-goers] have obviously voted with their feet, they are interested in seeing the film and we don't see why a faceless four people should be telling [them] what they shouldn't and cannot go see.'

Paul Coulter, a cinema director in Australia, on the banning of Baise Moi

✖ 'The real issue is not that this 18 certificate film could be viewed by prisoners generally, but that Stewart had not been identified as a prisoner who might require some special management or treatment.'

Nigel Giffin, QC, at the inquiry into the prison murder of Zahid Mubarek by cellmate Robert Stewart, a 19-year-old racist and 'psychopath', 48 hours after seeing Romper Stomper, a film about Nazi punks

❊ STATISTICALLY SPEAKING

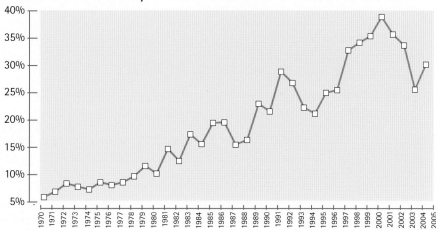

Number of films cut by UK censors between 1970 and 2004; Source: BBFC

CONFLICTING EVIDENCE?

'Should we ban bread because 90% of killers have eaten bread before their crime?'

Brian Miller, lawyer, Beyond Manhunt

'The Ancient Greek philosopher, Plato, advocated total censorship of one medium, because "It has a terrible power to corrupt even the best characters." The offending medium? Poetry.'

Tom Gormley, Cases in the Study of Media Effects

MORE TO THINK ABOUT

Some arguments for film censorship suggest that the passive viewer is more likely to be affected by a film than the active consumer of a book. Do you think this is true? Do books affect you more, or less, than films?

FIND OUT MORE: www.refused-classification.com www.zahidmubarekinquiry.org.uk
www.pre-cert.co.uk www.eirin.jp/english

37

Q: Does TV news over-simplify complex issues?

Reporters visit a hospital during a serious outbreak of a lung disease in China. Dramatic hospital scenes make exciting news stories.

NEWS PROGRAMMES on television present each item of news as a 'story'. The day's top stories are told with a combination of direct-to-camera speech, and film footage of events or people. Stories that are hard to provide footage for, or which feature no important personalities, may not 'feel' right for a main news programme. Dramatic stories such as violent crimes or disasters may 'feel' more urgent, with the excitement of being the very 'latest news'.

NO 'We don't do enough of the "new reader start here" explanation – 70% to 90% of an audience may not have a clue what's going on and that's absolutely the job of a news bulletin. We make big assumptions for audience understanding which simply isn't there.'

Tony Maddox, CNN Europe, News Xchange conference

✘ 'Sky News and the ITV News Channel – as well as all the American services like CNBC, CNN and Fox – actually provide good and professional news services for millions of people.'

Roger Mosey, Head of BBC TV News

YES

'The organisation of news for practical reasons encourages the adaptation of a convoluted way of simplifying events.'

David Altheide, author of Creating reality: How TV news distorts events

'[TV news is] coarser, shallower, more trivial, more prurient, more inaccurate, more insensitive, with each passing year ... a lot of thought seems to be going into making it thoughtless.'

Michael Buerk, journalist

✿ STATISTICALLY SPEAKING

- From 1990 to 1998, America's murder rate decreased by 20%. In the same period, the number of murder stories on network TV news increased by 600%.
- From 1983 to 1998, foreign news coverage in major US newspapers fell from 10% to 2% of the available space, while TV news coverage of foreign stories fell from 45% of news stories in 1975 to 13.5% in 1995.

✿ STATISTICALLY SPEAKING

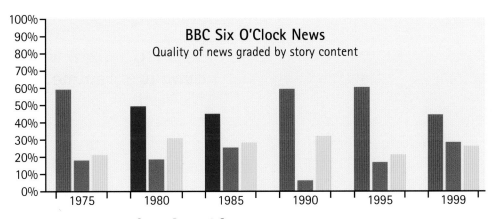

BBC Six O'Clock News
Quality of news graded by story content

Source: Barnett & Seymour

■ Broadsheet*
■ Tabloid*
▨ Foreign

*Broadsheet = Television news programming that features 'serious' stories.
*Tabloid = Television news programming that presents the news in a fast-paced, condensed form, usually with sensational material.

MORE TO THINK ABOUT

Many citizens of democratic countries are less interested in politics and current affairs, and are happy to limit their news intake to television news. Does this make them less informed? Should everyone read a newspaper, or should TV news become more 'serious'?

Q: Should we have TV cameras in courtrooms?

DEMOCRACIES PREVENT the state secretly imprisoning or executing people. Citizens can be involved in deciding who deserves punishment – as jury members. The public can also see people accused of crimes being treated fairly in court, through media reports. This helps citizens trust the state not to abuse their rights. Some people argue that TV coverage serves this aim too. Others say TV makes a circus out of justice.

US Superior Court Judge Rodney S. Melville imposed severe limits on the media for Michael Jackson's 2005 trial, to stop jurors being prejudiced by gossip before the trial. But the media discovered and reported some of the forbidden evidence.

YES

'Scotland allowed TV cameras access to civil and criminal hearings in 1992. The move was so hesitant that they did not permit live transmission. But even still, the resulting six-part BBC documentary looking at different trials and their backgrounds, shown in 1994 and repeated in 1996, made fascinating viewing and was a real insight into the workings of the law.'
Claire Fox, director of UK think-tank Institute of Ideas

'An enhanced public understanding of the judicial system is important in maintaining a high level of public confidence in the judiciary.'
131-1(a) of the Uniform Rules for the New York State Trial Courts, USA

'It's now quite accepted by the public. The reactions from the judges that I've spoken to are that it's working. There's certainly room for improvement in terms of what this can achieve but it's not having the adverse affects that some feared or predicted it would have. I feel that it benefits the society and its understanding of what happens in court and we need this if the public is to have confidence in the judiciary.'
Daniel Stepniak, University of Western Australia, assessing New Zealand's court TV experiment

NO 'When you change the audience, you change the proceeding ... The purpose of the court is not education or spectacle or public entertainment, but justice.'

George Gerbner, former dean of the Annenberg School of Communications, USA

✖ 'We were one step away from making our criminal justice system yet another reality TV show. I think that would have made voyeurism a substitute for criminal justice.'

County DA John Bradley, Texas, USA, after resisting the placing of a camera inside a jury room

✖ 'Someone is holding that camera, at certain angles, emphasising certain aspects of the trial. The end result is that conflicts between prosecutors and defense attorneys are exaggerated tremendously, since the audience is interested in heightened emotions and the dramatics of the trial. Attention is focused more on the participants of the trial and away from the evidence and the trial itself.'

Paula Fass, Professor of History, University of California, Berkeley, USA

❋ STATISTICALLY SPEAKING

• Since 1974 many states of the USA have conducted surveys to find out the effect of cameras on trials. Here are some of the findings:

Judges responses

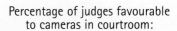

Percentage of judges favourable to cameras in courtroom:

100%

Arizona	82%
California	83%*
Nevada	75%

*64% said beneficial to the administration of justice

Percentage of judges believing cameras have no effect on conduct of trials:

Arizona	91%
New Jersey	94%

Lawyers' responses (California only):

Presence of the media and its equipment was not distracting:

84%

Presence of media personnel and their equipment did not affect the dignity of the proceedings:

64%

MORE TO THINK ABOUT

In democracies 'Justice must not only be done, but be seen to be done' – the public must be satisfied that the state only punishes those who clearly deserve punishment. So court cases must be reported, and accessible to public view. Why should TV reporting be treated differently? How much do you think cameras in courtrooms affect the participants: judges, jurors, lawyers, and defendants?

FIND OUT MORE: www.museum.tv www.courttv.com
http://dcaconsultation.twofourtv.com www.courttv.com/casefiles/simpson

Q: Will web media become more powerful than traditional media?

AMATEUR JOURNALISTS can create their own media on the Internet, setting up a weblog, or 'blog'. Trained journalists might be more careful to provide good information, and more aware of the ways that a story can mislead. But amateur journalists can dedicate themselves to following an issue that matters to them, in a way that few commercial media could afford to pay their staff to do.

YES ✓

'If the goal of opinion journalism is not ultimately money but influence and readers, the blogs are already breathing down the old media's neck.'

Andrew Sullivan, journalist and blogger

✓ '[US Senator Trent] Lott is in trouble because his [possibly racist] words were actually put in context [by bloggers]. It was a most democratic uprising – and showed the power of the Internet when it is truly free of the dependence on access, and the need to play nice with the powers that be.'

Arianna Huffington, US commentator

Before and during the 2003 invasion of Iraq, Western journalists found it hard to deliver serious news from Baghdad. The Baghdad Blogger, 'Salam Pax', won a worldwide following for his blog.

✳ STATISTICALLY SPEAKING

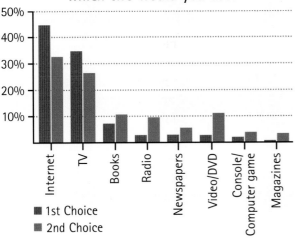

If you could only use two media, which two would you use?

- ■ 1st Choice
- ■ 2nd Choice

Source: Generational Media Study, September 2004, www.online-publishers.org

Top 15 economies, 2002, by Broadband Internet take-up

World Rank	Economy	Per 100 inhabitants	Change 2001-02	Total number of subscribers	% of all households
1	Korea (South)	21.3	24%	10,128,000	43%
2	Hong Kong, China	14.6	38%	989,000	36%
3	Canada	11.5	27%	3,600,000	20%
4	Taiwan, China	9.4	86%	2,100,000	31%
5	Iceland	8.6	138%	25,000	9%
6	Denmark	8.6	107%	462,000	16%
7	Belgium	8.4	90%	869,000	17%
8	Sweden	7.7	48%	693,000	13%
9	Austria	6.6	123%	540,000	14%
10	Netherlands	6.5	127%	1,060,000	19%
11	United States	6.5	46%	18,700,000	10%
12	Switzerland	6.3	308%	455,000	4%
13	Japan	6.1	176%	7,806,000	5%
14	Singapore	5.5	73%	230,000	20%
15	Finland	5.3	426%	274,000	8%

Source: International Telecommunications Union (ITU)

NO

'There is a danger that the hype about blogs can blind us to what is most interesting and stimulating about them: a good blog is a joy to read, providing a gateway to material you might never have found and provoking lively, informed debate. It doesn't have to tear down the world.'
Brendan O'Neill, The Times

❌ 'Blogging requires relatively little capital and is therefore not owned by a powerful few. Nonetheless, capital requirements exist and marginalise many groups. Furthermore, because blogging is almost entirely unprofitable, bloggers rely on power from other sources to support their activities. The result is a similar concentration of control.'
Robert Corr, Australian blogger

❌ 'Except for the very top hit-getting sites ... weblogs still need the validation of print and television media – otherwise it's just a bunch of people ranting away on the Internet, which is nothing new.'
'Atrios', top-10 blogger

MORE TO THINK ABOUT
Professional journalists investigate and write original stories. Bloggers usually refer only to stories already reported in other media. Do bloggers have more power when they discover a story, or when they investigate a reported story in more depth?

Glossary

Abortion medical procedure to end a pregnancy.

Advocate recommend, or push for something.

Allegedly when someone may have done something illegal or wrong but it has not been proved, for example, 'That's where he allegedly killed his wife.'

Ambiguous having more than one possible meaning.

Apathy lack of interest or energy.

Authoritative very reliable.

Bias an opinion or feeling that favours one side over another.

Boycott refuse to use, buy, or have anything to do with something.

Censorship controlling certain types of expression, usually of a sexual or political nature.

Citizen a person seen in their role as a rights-holding member of a society.

Civil libertarian a campaigner for civil liberties – rights which make democracy possible.

Commodity a product that is bought and sold in a market.

Consolidation when companies merge to make a bigger and stronger company.

Consumer a user of a good or service.

Controversy an argument or disagreement that has taken place over a long time.

Credibility trust earned by a person or organisation for truth and insight.

Cronie a close friend, especially someone you might favour above others.

Democracy a political system in which governments are elected by voters.

Diversity variety.

Empowerment given the power or authority to do something.

Explicit describing or representing sexual activity, or other sensitive material.

Fascist someone who supports a right-wing government that has strong social and economic control and is usually headed by a dictator. Fascists often favour their own indigenous population over immigrant groups.

Franchise exlusive ownership of something.

Free speech the right to express any viewpoint without censorship.

Government the group of politicians or other types of leader in control of a country.

Guise an outward manner or appearance put on in order to conceal something.

Hate speech a political term for expressions which cause offence, implying that speech 'is' violence.

Ideology a system of ideas and beliefs.

Incite to deliberately fuel a person or people into a particular action.

Independent not state-owned or part of a larger business.

Journalist any person paid to research, process or present information in the media.

Manifesto a public statement of the policies of a political party or government.

Mogul a very wealthy or powerful business person.

Niche market a particular part of the market for a product or service. It often has different requirements to the rest of the market and the product or service is designed to meet these needs.

Objectivity judgement based on real evidence that is uninfluenced by emotions or personal prejudices.

Overhead a cost of business, which includes buildings and fixed running costs.

Patronage the support of a powerful person, or 'patron'.

Perception a view of something, which may be differ from person to person.

Pernicious harmful.

Political correctness term for sensitive use of language – often overly so – eg about disabled people.

PR public relations: a promotion intended to create goodwill for a person or institution.

Prerequisite something required in advance of another thing, as a foundation for it.

Press (the) a traditional term for the media, referring to the machine that prints newspapers.

Prurient obsessed with sexual matters.

Racist treating people unequally in the belief that they should be defined by their 'race'.

Regime any system of control, or usually a system of government. It is often used to describe a government headed by a specific person or based on a particular ideology.

Revenue money earned.

Sceptical doubting or disbelieving.

Sovereign the freedom of choice and the right to participate with other citizens in running a government.

Submissive willing to submit to the orders or wishes of others.

Suppression forceful prevention; putting down by power or authority.

Survey research involving the gathering of data from many sources for analysis.

Values political or moral instincts, favouring one choice over another.

Weblog a website where users post informal journals of their thoughts and comments, which is updated frequently and normally reflects the views of the website's creator.

Whistleblower an informant.

Debating tips

WHAT IS DEBATING?

A debate is a structured argument. Two teams speak in turn for or against a particular question. Usually each person is given a time they are allowed to speak for and any remarks from the other side are controlled. The subject of the debate is often already decided so you may find yourself having to support opinions with which you might not agree. You may also have to argue as part of a team, being careful not to contradict what others on your side have said.

After both sides have had their say, and had a chance to answer the opposition, the audience votes on which side they agree with.

DEBATING SKILLS

1 Know your subject

Research it as much as you can. The debates in this book give opinions as a starting point, but there are website suggestions for you to find out more. Use facts and information to support your points.

2 Make notes

Write down key words and phrases on cards. Try not to read a prepared speech. You might end up losing your way and stuttering.

3 Watch the time

You may be given a set amount of time for your presentation, so stick to it.

4 Practise how you sound

Try to sound natural. Think about:
Speed – Speak clearly and steadily. Try to talk at a pace that is fast enough to sound intelligent and allows you time to say what you want, but slow enough to be understood.
Tone – Varying the tone of your voice will make you sound interesting.
Volume – Speak at a level at which everyone in the room can comfortably hear you. Shouting does not win debates. Variation of volume (particularly speaking more quietly at certain points) can help you to emphasise important points but the audience must still be able to hear you.
Don't ramble – Short, clear sentences work well and are easier to understand.

GET INVOLVED - NATIONAL DEBATING LEAGUES

Worldwide links
www.debating.net

Debating Matters, UK
www.debatingmatters.com

Auckland Debating Society, New Zealand
www.ada.org.nz/schlevels.php

Debaters Association of Victoria, Australia
www.debating.netspace.net.au

Index

advertisers 8, 9, 12, 14, 15
advertising 16, 17, 24
    ban 16, 17

Berlusconi, Silvio 4
bias 8, 11, 30, 44
BNP 32
books 4, 37
BSE 26
Bush, George W 10, 28

Campbell, Naomi 19
celebrities 18, 19
censorship 16, 32, 33, 36, 37, 44
children 6, 16, 17, 20, 21, 23, 34
citizens 4, 39, 40
    rights 9
civil libertarians 8, 44
Clear Channel 9, 12, 13
Coca-Cola 16
computer games 36
consumers 8, 13, 32, 44
courtrooms 18, 27, 40, 41
crime 40
cultural messages 24, 25

democracy 4, 10, 11, 12, 26, 28, 32, 39, 40, 41, 44
diet 17

extremists 32, 33

films 36, 37
Freedom of Information laws 26, 27
free speech 6, 32, 44

Gongadze, Heorhiy 6
governments 6, 8, 11, 12, 13, 26
    corruption 6

Harris, Jay 14
hate speech 7, 32, 33

information 6, 8, 9, 11, 12, 14, 15, 20, 21, 24
    sources of 19
Internet 5, 33, 36, 37, 42
Iraq 13, 27, 32, 34, 38, 42

journalists 6, 20, 21, 31, 42
juries 40

Kerry, John 10, 28, 29

laws 32, 33

media
    competition 12
    controls 7
    diversity 8, 30, 31
    ownership 12, 13
models 19, 24
Monaco, Princess Caroline of 18
Murdoch, Rupert 11
music 4, 8, 14

news 14, 18, 28, 30, 38
newspapers 4, 7, 8, 10, 12, 13, 14, 15, 18, 19, 20, 26, 28, 30, 36, 38, 39

paparazzi 18, 19
politicians 11, 26, 27, 28, 29
politics 10, 11, 12, 29, 39
    personality 28, 29
positive discrimination 30, 31, 45
press 9, 11, 12
privacy 18, 19
profit 15, 19

racism 30, 32, 42
racist speech 7
radio 9, 12, 13

secrecy 26, 27
self-esteem 24, 25
society 9
state, the 40, 41
Stern, Howard 9

television 13, 16, 22, 23, 24, 28, 34, 35, 36, 38, 39, 40, 41, 43
    coverage 10
    in courtrooms 40, 41

terrorists 6, 32, 33

violence 6, 33, 34
voters 4, 10, 11, 28, 29

web 42
weblogs 42, 43, 45
websites 8, 32, 42

Acknowledgements

The author would like to thank Freedom House (www.freedomhouse.org) for its survey data on political freedoms around the world, such as the Press Freedom Global Survey.

Picture credits: Oote Boe/Alamy: 22. Photofusion Picture Library/Alamy: 25. © Liu Dawei/Xinhua/Corbis: 38. © Vittoriano Rastelli /Corbis: 4. © Reuters/Corbis: 6, 34. Abaca Press/Abaca/Empics: cover, 19, 42. Santiago Llanquin/AP/Empics: 8. Phil Noble/PA/Empics: 32. Reed Saxon/AP/Empics: 13. photo Frank Fahrner: 31. Franklin Watts: 15. Toei/The Kobal Collection: 36. Last Resort Picture Library: 16. Stewart Cook/Rex Features: 40. Joe Raedl/Rex Features: 28. Sipa Press/Rex Features: 20. Sinclair Stammers/Science Photo Library: 26. Troy Witt/Take One Productions, Inc.: 14. TopFoto.co.uk: 11.

Text credits: Page 6: 1 'Stacy', Sydney IMC: http://sydney.indymedia.org/; 2 Mick Hume, 'Some last words on that libel trial, Last Magazine, Summer 2000; 3 Nadine Strossen, quoted in, 'We can never be safe - but at least we can be free'by Jennie Bristow, 15 November 2001: http://www.spiked-online.com/Articles/00000002D2C6.htm (12/9/05); Page 7: 1 Stanley Fish, There's No Such Thing as Free Speech and it's a Good Thing, Too (New York, OUP, 1994); 2 Rafe Mair, Vancouver Courier, 25 March 1998; 3 Peter Tatchell, quoted in 'Can music incite murder?' by Brendan O'Neill, 3 October 2004: http://www.spiked-online.com/Printable/0000000CA733.htm (12/9/05); Page 8: 1 Mike Walsh, 'Pass the Popcorn – it's the Six O'Clock News' 12 May 2003: http://fourth-estate.pmachinehosting.com/more.php?id=3_0_1_0_M2 (12/9/05); 2 John H. McManus, Market-driven Journalism: Let the Citizen Beware? SAGE Publications, 1994; 3 Anon, Spike Magazine, Hong Kong; 4 Augustine Edwards, Las Últimas Noticias; Page 9: 1 Council of Europe, Resolution 1003; On the ethics of journalism (1993); 2 Lord Reith, the first chairman of the BBC, 1924; 3 Adolf Hitler, dictator of Germany, 1940; Page 10: 1 Oliver Quiring, The Electoral Impact of Television's Unemployment Coverage in Germany, A Time Series Analysis 1994 – 1998 (2003); 2 DANIEL HENNINGER , 'How Dan Rather and the media's kings lost their crowns', Wall Street Journal, 12 November 2004; Page 11: 1 Polly Toynbee, 'The threat to our TV from this corrupter of politicians', The Guardian, UK, 30 April 2003; 2 Lord McNally of Blackpool, UK, in Hansard, 8th July 2003, 3 Pasuk & Baker, Political Change in Thailand, Ed: Kevin Hewison, Routledge, 1997; Jacob Stanley, BBC online Talking Point, 20 April 2005: http://news.bbc.co.uk/1/hi/uk_politics/vote_2005/frontpage/4466529.stm (12/9/05); Page 12: 1 Walter Cronkite, quoted in 'Creation of the Media Democracy Reform Movement' Robert W. McChesney and John Nichols, 12 November 2004; 2 Senator Hollings, Given at a Full Committee Hearing: 'Media Ownership: Radio Industry', 30 January 2003; 3 Aidan White, European Federation of Journalists, 2004; Page 13: 1 James Gattuso, The Myth of Media Concentration, www.heritage.org; 2 Professor Donna Logan, giving evidence to Canadian senators, 2003; 3 Communications Bill UK, 2000; Page 14: 1 Keynote address by Jack Fuller, President, Tribune Publishing Co. Poynter Institute Journalism and Business Values Conference, 20 January 2002; 2 Lowry Mays quoted in 'Media Moguls Pay No Rent for Using Our Airwaves' by Ralph Nader, 31 May 2003 by CommonDreams.org: http://www.commondreams.org/views03/0531-05.htm (12/9/05); 3 Code of Conduct for Directors, West Australian Newspapers Holdings Ltd; Page 15: 1 www.stateofthenewsmedia.org, 2005 report; 2 Tony Garnett, speech to the Drama Forum, London, 1997; 3 Lowell Bergman, 'Profit over public interest, again', 4 June 2002: http://thebigstory.org/features/insidestory.html (12/9/05); Page 16: 1 Senator Feargal Quinns, speaking at a Safefood seminar on the Broadcasting Commission of Ireland's new draft code on advertising to children, 21 April 2004; 2 Sue Kedgley MP , 'Urgent review of kids' advertising code needed, 27 March 2000: http://www.greens.org.nz/searchdocs/PR3135.html (12/9/05); 3 Strasburger, Victor C, Wilson, Barbara J, Children, adolescents and the media. Sage Publications: Thousand Oaks, CA, 2002; 4 Doctor Michael McDowell quoted in 'Advertising is child abuse, doctors say', 18 May 2004: http://www.abc.net.au/news/newsitems/s1110802.htm (12/9/05); Page 17: 1 Jeremy Preston quoted in 'Do Ads Make Children Fat?': http://www.waitrose.com/food_drink/wfi/foodissues/children/0402026.asp (12/9/05); 2 Widmeyer Communications survey, 2003; 3 Margo G. Wootan, Center for Science in the Public Interest, 2005; Page 18: 1 Tessa Mayes, Restraint or Revelation? www.spiked-online.com report, 2002; 2 Neil Wallis, speech given at a debate entitled 'Private Lives, Public People' at the London School of Economics, 7 March 2001; 3 ABC Newstore, USA; Page 19: 1 Naomi Campbell, quoted in 'Judges Nix Naomi's Court Victory' by Marcus Errico, 14 Oct 2002: http://www.eonline.com/News/Items/0,1,10676,00.html (12/9/05); 2 Lord Mostyn quoted in 'Lords calm fears of press curbs', Guardian, UK, 10 April 2002; Cari Ross quoted in 'Celebrities fight for privacy' By Donna Freydkin, USA Today, 7 June 2004: http://www.usatoday.com/life/people/2004-07-06-celeb-privacy_x.htm (12/9/05); Page 21: 1 Daniel Okrent, New York Times Ombudsman, 2004; 2 Hans-Martin Tillack quoted in 'Reporter who digs dirt on Eurocrats cops it from police' By Glenn Frankel, The Washington Post, 21 August 2004; 3 The National Union of Journalists (NUJ) UK, 29/01/04, www.nuj.org.uk; 4 Nicholas Jones, Sultans of Spin, Weidenfeld & Nicolson, 1999; 5 Kathleen Hall Jamieson quoted in 'Advocacy Groups Blur Media Lines' by Jeffrey H. Birnbaum, 6 December 2004: http://www.washingtonpost.com/wp-dyn/articles/A38184-2004Dec5.html (12/9/05); 6 Geneva Overholser, 'Anonymity: Father of Many a Sin', 29 May 2003: http://www.

poynter.org/column.asp?id=54&taid=35657 (12/9/05); Page 23: 1 http://www.parentstv.org/PTC/faqs/main.asp; 2 Robert Putnam, The strange disappearance of Civic America, PS, American Political Science Association, Winter 1995; 3 Michael Tchong, 'The New Family Ecosystem': http://www.fastcompany.com/resources/innovation/tchong/121304.html (12/9/05); 4 Andrew Jackson, Gail Fawcett, Anne Milan, Paul Roberts, Sylvain Schetagne, Katherine Scott,Spy Tsoukalas 'Social Cohesion in Canada: Possible Indicators', Social Cohesion Network, Department of Canadian Heritage , Department of Justice, November 2000; 5 Gentile & Walsh, National Survey of Family Media Habits 1999: www.mediafamily.org; Page 24: 1 Anne Becker quoted in, 'TV brings eating disorders to Fiji', 20 May 1999: http://news.bbc.co.uk/1/hi/health/347637.stm (12/9/05); 2 Mary Tannen quoted in 'The Democratisation of Beauty', by Christine Rosen, The New Atlantis, Number 5, Spring 2004, pp. 19-35. 3 Dr Allan Kaplan quoted in 'Dangers of dieting', Marilyn Linton, 24 February 2004: http://chealth.canoe.ca/columns.asp?columnistid=7&articleid=9856&relation_id=0 (12/9/05); Page 25: 1 Deanne Jade, Eating Disorders and the Media, National Centre for Eating Disorders, UK, 2002; 2 Patricia Karetzky, 'Femininity in Contemporary Asian Art': http://ca80.lehman.cuny.edu/gallery/femininity/essay.htm; 3 Polly Toynbee, 'Inequality is Fattening', The Guardian UK, 28 May 2004; Page 26: 1 Anne Kothawala, 'Time for the PM to End Ottawa's Culture of Secrecy', 6 Oct 2004: http://www.cna-acj.ca/client/CNA/CNA.nsf/web/Time+to+End+Ottawa's+Culture+of+Secrecy?OpenDocument (12/9/05); 2 David Banisar, The FreedomInfo.Org Global Survey, May 2004; 3 Mukelani Dimba, Open Democracy Advice Centre, 2002; Page 27: 1 Anthony Seldon, biographer of UK PM Tony Blair, reported in The Guardian UK, 11 January 2005; 2 Thomas Blanton, National Security Archive (USA), interviewed by Bill Moyers; Page 28: 1 William Schneider, 'Personality Politics Conquers Japan', The Atlantic, 8 August 2001; 2 David Gergen, 'Diplomacy is a Television Age: The Dangers of Teledemocracy' in Simon Serfaty, Ed, The Meida and Foreign Policy, New York: Foreign Policy Institue/St. Martin's Press, 1991, p50; Page 29: 1 Daunis Auers, 'Latvia's 2002 Elections', East European Constitutional Review, Winter/Spring 02/03; 2 Henry Graff, historian (USA), in 'Family Ties Play Key Role in 2000 Presidential Race', Baltimore Sun, 20 June 2000; 3 Preliminary Report on Monitoring of the Media Coverage of the Armenian Parliamentary Elections, May 1999; Page 30: 1 Ernest Sotomayor, Long Island Editor, Newsday.com, 10 August 2004: http://journalism.nyu.edu/pubzone/weblogs/pressthink/2004/08/10/unity_prez_p.html (12/9/05); 2 Dennis Greene, 31 Aug 2001: http://sport.guardian.co.uk/cricket/overbyover/story/0,10677,1556045,00.html (12/9/05); Page 31: 1 William McGowan, 'Colouring the News: How Crusading for Diversity has Corrupted American Journalism', CNN interview, 25 Jan 2002; Page 32: 1 Mark Bowden, The Atlantic magazine, 2004; 2 Margaret Thatcher, speech to the American Bar Association, 15 July 1985; Page 33: 1 US Bill of Rights, First amendment; 2 Laura Leets quoted in 'Sticks and stones may break bones, but words also hurt', by Kathleen O'Toole, 3 April 1998; 4 Ann Furedi, www.bpas.org.uk; 5 Article 19 position statement, in Striking a Balance: Hate Speech, Freedom of Expression and Non-discrimination, 1992; Page 34: 1 Charles Clarke quoted in 'Clarke: TV violence creates bullies' by Kamal Ahmed, The Observer, 28 December 2003; 2 James Ferman, quoted in The Sunday Telegraph, 19 May 1996; 3 George Gerbner, Annenberg School of Communications; Page 35: 1 Gene Mater, CBS, testimony to a congressional hearing, 1981; 2 Howard Gardner quoted in 'Networks Voice Views On Violence Research': http://www.medialit.org/reading_room/article515.html (22/9/05); 3 David Pearl, National Institute of Mental Health (NIMH), 1982; 4 Gene Jankowski, President, CBS Broadcast Group, 1985, cited on www.medialit.org; Page 36: 1 Natasha Cooper, crime novelist, Interviewed by Eve Tan Gee in Crime Time magazine; 2 letter from the CBFC quoted in 'Censor Board Bans "Final Solution"' By Kalpana Sharma, The Hindu, 6 August, 2004; 3 John Beyer, 'Corrupting Public Morals', Catholic Herald, 27 Aug, 1999; Page 37: 1 Paul Coulter quoted in 'Australian cinemas fight film ban', 13 May 2002: http://news.bbc.co.uk/2/hi/entertainment/1984117.stm (22/9/05); 2 Nigel Giffin, in an interview, 19 November 2004: http://www.zahidmubarek inquiry.org.uk/article.asp?c=387&taid=2928 (22/9/05); 3 Brian Miller, 'Beyond Manhunt', featured in MCV, August 2004; 4 'Ruination once again' – Cases in the study of media effects, Tom Gormley, www.theory.org.uk; Page 38: 1 Tony Maddox, CNN Europe, News Xchange conference, Slovenia, 2002, www.rts.org.uk; 2 Roger Mosey, 'Dumbing Down or Wisening Up', 24 November 2003; Page 39: 1 David Altheide, 'Creating reality: How TV news distorts events', Sage, 1976; 2 Michael Buerk quoted in 'Why Are We Dumbing Down The News?', Antonia Zerbisias: http://www.commondreams.org/views05/0301-29.htm (22/9/05); Page 40: 1 Claire Fox, 'This is one fly-on-the wall experiment we should encourage.' 12 January 2001: http://www.spiked-online.com/Articles/00000000542A.htm (22/9/05); 2 131-1(a) of the Uniform Rules for the New York State Trial Courts; 3 Daniel Stepniak, University of Western Australia; Page 41: 1 George Gerbner quoted in 'Cameras in the Courts: A Dissent', Andrew V. Siracuse and Michael Steinberg: http://amsir.home.isp-direct.com/Contents/Cameras_in_ct.html (22/9/05); 2 County DA John Bradley quoted in, 'Texas Court Keeps Out "Frontline" Cameras', Mary Alice Robbins, 18, Feb 2003; 3 Paula Fass, Professor of History, University of California, Berkeley; Page 42: 1 Andrew Sullivan, andrewsullivan.com; 2 Arianna Huffington, ariannaonline.com; Page 43: 1 Brendan O'Neill, The Times (London), 6th July 2003; 2 Robert Corr: http://robert.redrag.net; 3 'Atrios' atrios.blogspot.com